A WOMAN AND A MAN,
ICE-FISHING

A WOMAN AND A MAN, ICE-FISHING

Lee Rudolph

Texas Review Press
Huntsville

FIRST EDITION, 2006

Requests for permission to reproduce material from this work should be sent to:

Permissions
Texas Review Press
Box 2146
Sam Houston State University
Huntsville, TX 77341-2146

ACKNOWLEDGMENTS

"A Woman and a Man, Ice-Fishing" was published in the *New Yorker*.
"Heart's Desire", "The Man in the Bed", and "Aubade" were published in *Clark Now*.
"Acknowledgments and Disclaimers", "Another Letter" (as "Letter"), and "Little Prayer" were published in *The Church House Anthology*.
"Cockeast Pond: A Change of State" was published in the magazine *Spinner* and reprinted in the anthology *Contemporary New England Poetry* (Paul Ruffin, George P. Garrett, and X. J. Kennedy, editors).
"A Stone in the Garden", "Leek Sketch", and "Weather Report" were published in *Coastlines*.
A version of the first two parts of "The Kidnapping of the President" was published in the New Bedford *Standard-Times*.
"Beauty" and "Fast Year" will be published in a forthcoming issue of *Momentum*.
"Dr. G., Riddled by an Old Friend" was published in *The Niagara Magazine* and reprinted in *The Country Changes* (Alice James Books).
"November" was published (as "November Beach") in the anthology *Mercy of Tides* (Margot Wizansky, editor).
"Big Bang" will be published in a forthcoming issue of the *American Journal of Physics*.

Cover photograph by Mark Wilson; sculpture photographed, *Man Discovering Something*, by Pat Keck.

Cover design by Paul Ruffin

Library of Congress Cataloging-in-Publication Data

Rudolph, Lee, 1948-
    A woman and a man, ice-fishing / Lee Rudolph.-- 1st ed.
        p. cm.
    ISBN 1-881515-80-X (alk. paper)
    I. Title.
    PS3568.U355W66 2005
    811'.54--dc22

                                                2005014260

A WOMAN AND A MAN, ICE-FISHING

CONTENTS

ICE-FISHING

WEATHER REPORT

WORD PROBLEMS

LITTLE PRAYERS

ICE-FISHING

A WOMAN AND A MAN, ICE-FISHING

She: cuts a disk of ice from his skull,
lets down the sinker and line, the hook and ladder,
making remarks on the cold. Lighting fires on the ice,
she sends more bait down the fishes' dumbwaiter.
And a tug on some line! A bell rings! Who can find
the right one in time? Lines trembling, profuse as axons.

He: makes coffee, several pots, one on each fire,
believes the Groucho Marx version of an executive's desk,
I refuse to speak to a fish,
Put him through to my secretary,
Don't call us, we'll call you.
The fish try to get through, all ring together.

And, together, they (the man and the woman) lower
thermoses of coffee and sacks of provisions
hand over hand as jute rope splinters pierce mittens.
A boy at the far end, out of a fakir's basket,
climbs as fast as they extend him more rope.
Sheikhs pursue him. He hollers,

Send bedsheets! And they pour him some down.
There are scimitars under the ice! And he emerges,
no stranger. The man melts and becomes a fish.

HEART'S DESIRE

What you do not have
you cannot lose;
what you possess,
you will lose over and over.

The ruin of a landmark
is a landmark,
its new name blooms
from the mode of its destruction.

Mother, you have been taken from me,
and oh! the taste of my loss
is sweeter than any milk
you ever spared.

The name of the stone
is Heart's Desire
but it is a stone
and it is a stone.

ACKNOWLEDGMENTS AND DISCLAIMERS

The man is a riddle he wants the woman to answer
and he wants her to be his mirror *how else* he says
*can I see myself   but you will move as you always
move   define your own life as always* he says
I only ask you to face me. This bores her:
I don't have a smooth surface.

OK (his answer comes from a long way off)
be my radio telescope. She busies herself
with the crèche on the card table, skews cotton batting drifts
around pipecleaner palms, pairs off the folk
animals out of her archives: elephants, armadillos,
thicknecked swans whittled from bars of soap

inexpertly (real antiques). No family. No kings.
The swans float on a pink mirror. The house is so warm.
His voice spins on the turntable: *how many grooves
does an LP have on one side?* She's not bad
at reading labels in motion: a bit of a palmist too: she knows
there's only one groove, spiraling down to silence,

and a lifeline on each hand, and not enough time to read
between every card in the deck and still keep house.
I see you she sighs *I knew you were there all the time.*

AN ESTATE SALE

If she hadn't already known
it would have been clear
this is his family reunion:
everyone here
she recognizes without a photograph album

    (or an introduction:
    he wandered off
    even before the auction
    began), the light of his self
    refracted as by a prism into its spectrum.

Here's a pile of old guidebooks
to elsewhere, inadequate,
obsolete as these slide rules
or that Depression *Etiquette.*
(He'd said he'd rely on having been there before,

    would count on his fingers
    to pick old locks
    though now the doors were strangers'
    and the penciled marks
    marked strange children's heights on the frame of
        each known door.)

She wanders tent to tent, among
trestle tables, a red boxcar
barn, gummy whitewashed tree trunks
in the hornets' orchard
(where hard hollowed peaches hum), along the road—
        oiled dirt—

down to the farm pond:
children are rowing
and bailing. And shouting? The sound
cuts out. There's no knowing,
without subtitles, what's the plot of this picture:

is a child about to drown
or at least be held under
(by cousins it's never known)
in the algae-veiled water?
Is a flood coming, like the one that stained the parlor

wallpaper, ruined its
fruitwood wainscoting,
left jars of pen-nib pitted
cherries and pickled onions bobbing
out of the coal-hole chute (freed from the fruit cellar),

rusted the upright's strings
and unglued its keys' veneer
while they were waiting
things out on the second floor?
(No one in the family sings or plays: nobody here.)

Or is there no plot
to these home movies, as there is no album?
Each snapshot
in the jumbled shoebox
could fit into a story anywhere, or nowhere.

PRESERVES

Dick's father died suddenly one August Monday
a year after the war. Sunday, his wife and he
had driven out into the country for peaches;
they'd bought two bushels. Dick remembered the Tuesday
by smell. All day, women from up and down the street
filled Mason jars with preserves, and as the jars cooled
Dick took them down to the cellar for his mother.
Dick went to college, then to divinity school.
There were other wars. His sister who stayed at home
reported to him how—maybe every second
July or August—a jar would explode in the
dark, in the heat. She'd clean up. One
                          summer Sunday,
visiting, Dick went down and threw out what
                          was left.

ESCAPE READING

1. *The bare plot.*   2.*The longer story*

When I was a boy A Saturday summer night in Pike Run Township,
                Pennsylvania, near the Monongahela:
we read science my father; my uncle Ollie, a coal miner
    fiction,   (dying of black lung—nobody knows yet);
                a boy, ten years old. Talking science fiction
I and my father, on the porch, in two swings.
                                    The husbands smoke
we lived on two Lucky Strikes, which Mean Fine Tobacco,
    spaceships, which smell of raisins. The boy's time machine
                is powered by cellophane, only big enough
two different   to send small messages out on the tide of time
    planets.   planets: from his desert planet. My father,
                empassioned, explains that when you read you must
dangerous aliens. see, feel, and taste, "taste the chocolate ice cream"
                the author described. What's threatening in this
Mother read   first lesson in literature, from a smart man
    mysteries.   thwarted? Small messages. *LS/MFT. Save me*

I went to college, Where is my mother in this picture? It is her
                house: that is, she was born in it, suffered
became a detective typhoid fever in it ("my belly was black-and-blue
                and I lost all my hair"), fought in it with her
story fanatic,   mother and her sister, and left them in it
                to go to college, study chemistry, get work
I read them by series at American Steel & Wire during the war, and now
                the three of them, in the kitchen, wash the dishes,
where anyone can die and my grandfather, the retired machinist
                with no spittoon next to his basement lathe
but the detective. though machinists (and chemists) all chew tobacco,
                is dying in bed upstairs, his larynx missing.

Then my father	The Cleveland Clinic taught him to croak some words
died.	the summer before. He writes on a Magic Slate.
	My father and I are visiting, with my mother,
	from Cleveland, where we live. A thwarted woman.
Freed, my mother	My mother does not read science fiction. She read
	Horatio Alger, *Billy Whiskers, Five Little Peppers,*
escaped to Samoa,	in her sickbed. When her father was too ill to read
	he gave me his *Scientific Americans.*
Pakistan, China.	I found his *Home Study Guides*: to *Logarithms,*
	Use of the Slide Rule, Reinforced Concrete.
When she's home	He is an inventor, but he holds no patents,
she reads	cannot make a time machine; and I have lost mine,
	I cannot reach back, or answer the small message
autobiographies.	unless time is a closed curve (knot untying itself
	in the fourth dimension) and this flashlight I wave
I read	at the night sky of winter (which swallows it)
mathematics	is the miner's headlamp, is the cobalt treatment, is
	the sun through the blue square of cobalt glass
and Earl Stanley	the day of the eclipse—too bright to look at
Gardner.	long, too bright not to see with my eyes closed.

THREE MEN, SPEAKING

"When I was half the age I am,"
said the middle-aged man in a borrowed voice,
"I dreamed no future, I held no past,
I froze in a present bright as ice.
        Now listen to me."

"If I was as big as they were then,"
said the boy-child wearing his father's face,
"no one would bruise, no one would blister,
no one would burn down anyone's house.
        Couldn't they see?"

The old man is a bundle of clothes,
false teeth, bifocals. Empty shoes.
"When and if," the lost son said,
in the hard dry light, to the creaking crows.
        "Where, oh where am I?"

THE MAN IN THE BED

The man in the bed, who does not know
what the dream said, who does not knot
the sheets to escape from the fire in his head

but lies flat, pale and white, in moonlight—
stripes slipping between the slats
of the blind (while Saturn and Jupiter meet

as it seems from his bedroom)—does not sleep.
He is thinking: of blue stains on a porcelain sink
under the hot-water tap; blue gas

flames; the blue of an empty sky
with a pale moon rising, paler than cloud;
net of blue veins crossing a pale breast.

At midnight, color has drained away,
the moon is invisible over the roof.
What, what did the dream say?

WEATHER REPORT

COCKEAST POND: A CHANGE OF STATE

New Year's Eve. Warm spell begins to break.
The wild swans' pond (near the line of summer
houses with their shutters nailed closed,
empty for winter) is beginning to ice over:
the mystery of a change of state:
how is it that what is ice was water?

The houses have two views of water,
ocean and pond. Storms' wind-driven waves break
against them; no more may be built, the State
and prudence forbid it. In great storms of summer,
dying hurricanes, some have fallen over.
They are not rebuilt. The Town's deed-book stays closed.

The houses have two views, but have been closed
since sometime after Labor Day. By then, the water
is cold, and the winds are colder, blowing over
cold sand. The wild rose bushes do not break
the wind. Some owners come back after summer
for a few weekends, but live out of state

and find five hours on the Interstate,
each way, too much; and if it rains, you're closed
up with the kids all weekend, not like summer
when they have friends there. Anyway, the water
is just too cold.—When the milkweeds break
no one in the houses sees their silk float over.

No one is in the houses. Shuttered over,
their windows are blind to the changing state
of things: the clumsy taxiing, the noisy break
from pond to air of a wild swan; the closed
pod that opens; light floating on the water;

fall turning to winter, as it had turned from summer.

New Year's Eve. It does not seem that summer
has ever been, that winter will be over,
ever. A warm spell has only meant the water
in the swans' pond is not yet ice: a state
of grace: the year's accounts will soon be closed.
Who knows, once ice has formed, when it will break?

Winter locks things up, keeps them safe under
the ice. It is not the season to suggest
openings. There must be time for things to mend.

A STONE IN THE GARDEN

I was born (as I later learned) on Easter
    in earliest spring, at noon,
while snowfall dulled the peals of the churches' bells
    and stalled the trolleys in drifts.
I have been on earth, and in time, forty years,
    my father dead nearly half,
my tears mostly unshed and my eyes dried tight.

In blue dawn this Easter, I heard new birds sing;
    then, under hay in its trench,
I found the first asparagus, one thick inch
    of scaly tip, rose and green.
The stalk had grown round a stone, learning its curve;
    that obstruction left behind,
the tip was still crooked. The curve was its own.

Months fit poorly into years; the Church's moon
    waxes and wanes on paper;
Easter was later this year, so I'm fully
    my age, among vegetables
—leeks, asparagus, parsnips—seeking some light,
    or warmth. I walk to the house
through the shadow of the rose bush, drawn in frost.

How did the stone get into the trench? How deep
    was it? I didn't know, I
was afraid to disturb the root by digging.
    Should I just let the stone lie?
Should I try to get the stone out of the ground?
    Is the gift of tears useless
now, bitter and late, the past an empty tomb?

LEEK SKETCH

In flower now, a last year's leek (left all
winter in the garden) has become
a center of the bumblebees' attention,
five or eight at once on it. They may not see
how part of it, part of the sky, are the same pale
lavender; they see things differently.

LETTERS FROM EXILE

1.

The city is empty without you.
I spend many hours each day in the museum,
where there has been a scandal! I wonder
if you remember their prize exhibit,
the "Landscape with Gray Eminence"? What murk!
They cleaned it for the Exposition—and now we see
it is "Psyche and Eros"! The signature seems genuine,
but all the guidebooks have had to be rewritten.
I wish you were here, to give your opinion.

2.

How we thought we knew the city!
And so we did. Still, I have found places
we never saw (I *think* you never saw them):
a cave where some children lived; a pile of rats' bones.
But that was long ago, before things changed.
I have not gone back to that quarter again.

3.

She is leaning over him.
Clean sheets surround him.
He may be asleep, or wondering
how he got into that bed.
Maybe it's snowing outside.
Somewhere there is a wonderful blank.

Do you remember our first visit?
You kept our ticket stubs, and the curator

gave you *carte blanche.* Years later he ran amuck
with his bucket of bleach, wanting to clean
all the rest of the pictures. You were no longer here.
The city is empty. I think of you often.

ANOTHER LETTER

I found your last letter to me again today,
pressed and creased in the old dictionary
I haven't consulted for years:
I am fluent enough: what words
I do not know are words I do not want to know.

The letter is dry, brittle as a pressed flower.
The dictionary smells sweet as a rotting stump.

You wrote me, I thought, in another language.
Today I recognize it as my own.

LULLABY

I dreamt my shoes were white with graveyard dust.
No one I know is dying, I've never seen
any graveyard that wasn't green;
here they're all grassy and green.

I dreamt my eyes were wet with graveyard mud—
when I woke I was crying, singing a song
about a revolution, how it went wrong.
Why does it always go wrong?

    This   is the end   of history,
    dust and mud, rust and blood,
    no more sleep   for me,
    sleep   for me.

I dreamt   people next door, no teeth of their own.
What they eat   is soft and sweet,
borrow teeth   to chew their meat,
bellies filled with stones.

I dreamt   people downstairs, no beds of their own—
where do they sleep,   where do they sleep?
Go to sleep,   go to sleep,
go to sleep and don't dream.

    This   is the end   of history,
    dust and mud, rust and blood,
    no more sleep   for me,
    sleep   for me.

PORTRAIT OF Y.

I want to control my dreams
the tense neck of the dark girl screams
(for anyone, who will look, to see)
though she mouths another vocabulary
aloud: "I want to get in touch
with my body and with my dreams."
What I see is her clutching hand.

Call it greed:
emptiness, aching to be filled;
but nothing can be enough. It feeds
insatiably, and cannot digest.

*My dreams are **mine**, they are part of **me**;*
I will force them, I will force myself,
to behave. To have good orgasms: to breathe:
to learn what is natural, and do it—
always with threats of force.

She learns
what is natural from the authorities
(only the best), she wears her face
in a perpetual sulk, and heavy-
lidded and lipped, like a puzzled child
unsure whether to cry.

If, finally, only the greed survives,
what will become of her unshed tears
in her lost black eyes?

SOLSTICE SONG

>   Please don't   leave   me,
>   if you do, I don't know
>   how I'll get along.
>   Please   don't you   leave me,
>   if you do, I don't know how
>   I'll manage when you're gone,

>   'cause it took so long to get here,
>   and it's been so hard to stay,
>   and it took so long,
>   and it's been so hard,
>   and now you say you're going to go away
>   again,
>   now you say you're going to go away.

I phoned the Weather Bureau
to ask them for the forecast,
they said today would be
the shortest day of the year.
They said there'd be a little snow
but the sky would not be overcast,
they said tonight would be the longest night
because you are not here.

>   Please don't   leave me,
>   if you do, I don't know
>   how I'll get along.
>   Please don't you   leave me,
>   if you do, I don't know how
>   I'll manage when you're gone,

>   'cause it took so long to get here,
>   and it's been so hard to stay,

and it took so long,
and it's been so hard,
and now you're fixing to go away
again,
now you're fixed to go away.

I phoned the operator
to ask for her assistance,
I said I was having trouble
getting through to you.
She said, "You must try later, sir,
that number is long distance,
and storms have brought down all the lines,
nothing's getting through."

Please don't   leave me,
if you do, I don't know
how I'll get along.
Please don't you   leave me,
if you do, I don't know how
I'll manage when you're gone,

'cause it took so long to get here,
and it's been so hard to stay,
and it took so long,
and it's been so hard,
and now you've up and gone away
again,
now you've up and gone away.

WEATHER REPORT

I cannot speak for you
and I have nothing to say
except that it is raining:
another terrible day.

You cannot speak for me,
although "we" is thick in your mouth;
eyes and ears in a bubble of gas,
you cannot see how I take each breath

all by myself. We cannot speak.
This is simple, terrible fact;
weather we live in;
play we act.

WORD PROBLEMS

THE KIDNAPPING OF THE PRESIDENT

1970
                                    I meant
the kidnapping *by* the President, of course.
He took all of us hostage, he had his bombs
in that room where he and we were together,
he had certain demands. But it was a ploy:
like us, he had read the reports, listened to
certain genuine victims' accounts of love
they grew to feel for their captors; he wanted
us to love him. Only that.

1980
                            Some of us were
kidnapped by our parents.—How did I mean this?
Not literally, not at first, not until
I met a child whose father gathered him up
once, into his arms, and ran: ran out of the
playground, out of the mother's sight, out of the
neighborhood. She went to court to get the boy
back. What is it like, to be so desired?
Is it like living in a room full of bombs?

1999

Later, fallen from a window, the boy died.
Later yet: much later: in fact, now, in his
windowless room, a president is holding
himself for ransom. There are many of him.
I cannot keep up with the news, history,
my birthdays. The mother gave away the boy's
undamaged organs, they were small and useful,

and I assume they persist, seventeen years
after his fall, naturalized, in bodies
that know them nearly as well as they know the
backs of their hands.

YOU HAVE A PROBLEM

You have a problem, so you want to solve it.
It is so ugly, anyway, with that mean face
that (as we say) only a mother could love it.

Differential diagnosis: a *bad habit*
is not a *neurosis*, which is not *madness*;
you have a *problem*, so you want to solve it.

Clarify your relationship! Do you have it?
Does it have you? Are you both in a bad place?
That (as we say) only a mother could love it

is axiomatic: you will never leave it
till you can bear it, nor can it release
you. Have a problem? So? You want to solve it?

You think you can use acid to dissolve it
to particles, or burn it, or freeze it whole in ice?
That? As we say, only a mother could. Love it!

You'll get nowhere with that knife. If you halve it,
you know how both halves will grow back up. Yes,
you have a problem, so you want to solve it;
well, as we say, only a mother could love it.

BEAUTY

Intimate with her *bête noire*
at last (no mastery; no mask),
what can she do but ask?
"Beast, show who you are."

He'd thought he was bare.
"No, silly, that's skin.
I want to see *in,*
where the bones are."

FAST YEAR

Winter blinks; before you focus
on it, Spring sprints past—the crocus,
daffodil, and tulip die back,
bloom and perfume leave the lilac;

Summer comes, the die is cast,
grab those roses while they last!
A thorn can hurt worse than a splinter;
late Fall festers into Winter.

DR. G., RIDDLED BY AN OLD FRIEND

The acid logician,   his old friend, is living
at the end of a street   hung with bunting and wreaths.
Yet the house has a porch. "This is like our childhood,"
the visitor tells him,   walking through the front door.

But, nothing is the same. Neighbors bury bathtubs
upright, drain-holes in earth, to make shrines for Mary.
Theories—economies   shrinking, big bangs, black holes
and the heat-death coming sooner to this corner

than that (all statistics, in the mechanical
universe)—don't explain facts, brought home like skim milk.
This is Philadelphia!   not summer vacation.
There are no mailboxes   here, they talk face-to-face.

"What is it, farther than stars, its edges ragged
as drifted continents'?" "Is it the other half
of the map, the marked bill, the torn social contract?
"No. Look in the watched pot. Take it straight from the mouth

of the baby. The gift   is fear. It's easier
to keep the camel's nose out of your business
The unexamined horse   is not worth giving." "No."
...How can they find common ground, who have been so far

apart, for so long? They   sift circumstance, gossip,
everyday dirt, gently   as archaeologists:
unpack and pack china   wrapped in Sunday comics,
rotogravures, like two   surgeons, like a jukebox,

one record at a time: until no room is left
in the visitor's case.   (It is a black bag, he
thought it could hold any   thing, that's why he become
a doctor.) "The world is   the place for *everything*,

and everything is in   its place. But the little
individual *things*,   I worry about them."
"The world is a black box."   When the visit is done
these two old friends walk down   to the corner together.

WORD PROBLEM

The acid logician (an algebra teacher)
is having a birthday. As old as his father
(that old dog, of many names: *A.*, with a bathtub
which he fills at rate x as it drains at rate y;

K., foreman of a crew of forlorn ditchdiggers;
even *Q.*, trying to row his boat down the stream
gently, while headwinds and currents fight for control)
was, when their ages' sum was double their difference

and their differences (more even than now) burnt holes
in every tablecloth, clogged all the sinks with muck,
he has invited just one guest, his riddling friend,
to whom he explains: "You can take a slow bull to

a china shop, but you can't make him take himself
seriously, by the horns." Then it's ice cream and cake;
one candle to grow on. "A fish of a different
kettle"...not much of an answer, but all he gets

while his friend is chewing things over. As they move
to the presents (mostly from himself), his friend speaks:
each man sets his own price in the fleamarket of
ideas; Everyman is for himself; it's not

just a matter of taste who's overboard with (first)
the rats, then the children. "Diogenes! Do you
remember? *That dog is your dog. That dog is a*
father. Therefore..." but he can't seem to master his

voice, and neither completes   the syllogism. "Don't
shoot fish in the barrel   you're living in. I brought
this for you." The smallest   of gifts, the end of the
alphabet, it falls through   the dark, a singing lamp.

AN INVITATION TO SPEAK

This poem is talking to itself.
If you overhear it
on the sidewalk
leave it alone.

This poem is propaganda.
If you overhear it
through the wall,
tear the wall down.

This poem is an invitation.
If you overhear it
from the next room,
open the door
and come in.

ENTRE NOUS

The mutton in its mint sauce has
no longing for blue sky, green grass;
the *entrecôte au poivre vert*
is ignorant of black despair—
so we assume, carnivorous,
eating what is set before us.

SCRAPS FROM THE DREAM NEWSPAPER

Retired from the   public life
of   foreign   service   —
oubliettes and abattoirs — his
private   heart   remembers
nothing that his blood forgets.
Magical,   musical   memoirs,
these have been   written by a
man whose life is still subject
to threats   though he   lives
surrounded by a net of   dikes.

**When parachuting for sport in the mountains
always remember: at the first sight of water,
even of ice, control your descent.   Keep dry.
Take the first road home.**

"We used to   call it   The Boxes.   The
mills were here." reached it by cycling
over oakleaves in half-sunlight in the
underground woods "during the war.
Now it's the new student lounge."

*In the fire station   back room   on the wall
all   the   alarm boxes   of the city were
represented by   blue cones of gas
flame. Long after the   air raids and firestorms,
the pilot   testified   a gas beacon
had guided   his bombardier.*

It was the war within the peace, God in the mighty fortress-machine, everything under the surface: you couldn't know which trees were reinforced with steel trunks. And whatever voice we heard croaking orders and proverbs out of the earth ... well of course it had to be God's.

KUNSTMUSEUM

1. *Der Triumph des Todes* (after Pieter Breughel the Elder)

In The Triumph of Death, who's smiling? (Death's-heads
                                        don't count.)

        The king, in the lower lefthand corner, isn't smiling.
        A skeleton pins his shoulder to the ground
        with one arm; its other bony hand
        holds an hourglass to his face.
        The king looks worried,
        but doesn't focus on the sand:
        what gets him down's the second skeleton
        rifling his barrels of gold, wearing his crown
        or the skeleton of his crown.

        The courting lovers at the lower right
        might be smiling. And why not? The lute
        he's playing as he sings to her
        is tunefully accompanied
        by a skeleton's bowed viol
        over their shoulders, where they are not looking
        just at the moment.

                None of the crowd
        of peasants and burghers, being driven and drummed
        into a hobnailed boxtrap by a skeleton army
        who bear swords and trumpets, who are led by one
        skeleton mounted on a long thin horse,
        are smiling: they are screaming. And the priest,
        and the gentle ladies fleeing a disrupted feast,
        plucked at and embraced by skeletons (as another,
        wearing a red cape, serves them a skull on a silver platter),
        and the gentlemen fleeing all the other way,
        and the single fool in motley underneath the table,

aren't smiling either.

But the second horse,
long and thin as the first, in blinders,
hitched to the wagon full of skulls,
bearing on his back a magpie and a skeleton
that waves a lantern and a bell, smiles
as a horse can smile: his muzzle kisses
the peasant woman on the ground
before the cart—and she, on her knees,
has turned her head back to the horse,
her hair is in the dirt, she's looking up
into his big horse eyes, she's smiling
the biggest smile

in all this hell.

2. *Basler Meister von 1487*

Salzburger Meister; Meister der Aarhusen Passion;
Basler Meister; Bayerischer Meister; Tiroler Meister.
In this first room I see no suffering, not really:
only the Passion, the bloodless birth
of John the Baptist, Mary on her deathbed.
Her eyes sink, her skin is gray, but I see no one suffering
except for one wild man crying in the foreground
—that's about it. In this world,
there are no trees, ships, cities, in the background:
it's all gold, red brocade, egg-shell-blue sky.

Through the next door, a diptych by the Basler Meister
of 1487: Hieronymous Tscherkkerbürlin at 16,
alive in the left-hand panel, dead at the right
with leather worm-ridden skin on his arms and chest
and a bare skull still bearing some of his golden hair.

3. *Die Lorelei*

Walking out into the city, I find myself singing.

Ich weiß nicht, was soll es bedeuten, daß ich so traurig bin...

Und ruhig fließt der Rhein, through Basel, down to the summer sea.

(Basel, May 1998)

NOVEMBER

Though banks of dark clouds hid the sun,
it was being pointed at, not subtly,
by the whole sky, which might as well have been
a medieval panel with a gold leaf glory
pointing at the blank wood in its center
where some saint's face has flaked away.

No matter that there is no face: if we are clever
we can tell which saint it is—the robes, the flower
at the feet, the instrument of torture
and martyrdom, the mascot (dog, lion, bird)...
any one of these is better than a signature,
if we have learned to read; although the painter
has and had no signature, no name.

God has hidden his face,
to which the whole creation points,
somebody said. I follow my own footprints
back up the beach, to look a second time
at the sea-snails' elegant, idiot scrawl
on the sandy bottom of the tidal pool.

LITTLE PRAYERS

To say deliberately just how it is with me is apparently
how I pray, if I may judge by the language that
comes to me—especially when I am at a loss for grief,
confusion, gratitude, or fear. In moments of impasse—
but only when I have earned the right to say it because
I have tried hard—I have written 'Creator Spirit, come.'

Paul Goodman, *Notes for a Defense of Poetry*

LITTLE PRAYER

Creator Spirit, who,
blessing with excess
of ripe fruit, split the peach tree
from crotch to root,

protect me from success
as the world knows it.
Also from my bitter smugness: I do long
for sweetness, lost. Poison ivy

mounds where the tree was.
When I want peaches
I buy them, and every next spring
find in the compost split and sprouting pits.

LITTLE PRAYER ON ST. VALENTINE'S DAY

The sculptor removes what isn't
statue from the stone block;
      the composer remembers the tune
      before writing down the first note.

Creator Spirit, is love
what we work at? or what
      comes to us, whole,
      though we live in it blind and deaf?

AUBADE

Look, love, over the flat fields:
the winter sun
rises out of the southeast, red;
first colors return, then dawn.

No. I will watch the west. The moon
has been swept up in a brush of black trees,
it has been full, and must go down
just now, as you watch the sun rise.

SNOW PRAYER

I had taken the word of the calendar
and slept, thinking winter was over.
      Morning came: the sky was gray,
      it had nothing to say;

the garden was hidden beneath a new drift,
still dead. I have lost something I loved,
      but what, and when,
      I have forgotten.

If I could remember, I could make an end:
let me remember. By afternoon
      the snow was gone, in wind,
      in untrustworthy sun.

WIND PRAYER

     A friend writes: she is moving on,
       love is not enough. When gorges yawn
let her float lightly, spider borne on silk,
unwebbed, a single drifting thread. If talk

     bruises her, let all be still;
       contrariwise, if—after all
the music—silence hurts, let her hear (one
by one) the shaped notes rise into attention,

     emerge from chaos into chorus.
       Let her attend. Attend her. ... Is
anyone there? Only the wind: the breath
of the world, voice in its throat, updráft.

LITTLE PRAYER IN NOVEMBER

That I am alive, I thank
no one in particular;
and yet am thankful, mostly,
although I frame no prayer

but this one: Creator
Spirit, as you have come,
come again, even in November,
on these short days, fogbound.

LITTLE PRAYER IN LATE FEBRUARY

Alive still. Long nights
shorter than the nights before,
short as All Hallow's Eve
the dead end of October.

Hollowed, full of light,
had my creation what life
I gave it, less, or more? Lamp-skull
carved with a light touch: alive, still.

BIG BANG

Don't speak to me, lightning: I'll hide
where you can't find me, under my bed,
as the hair on my arms rises, the dust-
bunnies cling; till you shake the floor, slow-voiced.

Astronomers stare. Their eyes are so big,
they can see so long ago. A cracked egg-
shell of heat-lightning frames the oldest sky
in all directions. Thunder, pass me by.

ACCOMMODATION

   I am nearly fifty. My eyes, always weak,
        now fail me far and near. Is that a tick,
small as a pepper-grinding? Over there,
still at the field's border: bush or deer?

   Author of symmetry, grant (as I grope
        again for my other pair of glasses) hope
when I am hopeless; light, in the fearful dark;
and scale, to know the fixed star

                        from the breaking spark.

SO THERE'S THIS DRUNK,

see, crawling around
underneath a lamppost: you all know the punchline:
"Because the light is so much better here!"
                                        Blackout.

But: if he keeps searching
in the light, on his knees,
something might turn up, something
of even greater interest than his keys.

But: if, down the street, in dark
too thick to tell two cats apart,
he finds keys and cannot tell whose keys they are,
he might open who knows what unexpected door.

SECOND PERSON SINGULAR

Trickster, Whose creation is
    like a game of pick-up-sticks
primed into chaos to explode
at touch, and yet can be teased out

    by bits with patience or with luck,
        is chaos not Thy very fact
from which Thou dost tease us to see
what we may make of Thee?

A DRY-STONE DIKE

This wall is just to use stones up,
it marks no boundary, pens no sheep;
     still I build it strong and flat
     and seek what chink each stone might fit.

Day by day, as stone by stone,
I make do. It is not done.
     Is anyone there?—No answer.
     I do without an answer.

Notes:

Page 42: "I don't know what it means that I am so sad. . . . And the Rhine flows silently." (Hermann Hesse)

Page 55: I now have very good bifocals.

Page 56: Dedicated with thanks to Gordon Fitch, whose offhand allusion to the eponymous joke sparked the poem.

Page 58: Many unmortared walls (dry-stone dikes) in the fields and second-growth woods of southern New England are "consumption walls," built where they are because it was easier to pile up the stones left by the glaciers than to haul them off.